Conversation

Also by Stephen Ratcliffe

POETRY

New York Notes (Tombouctou, 1983)

Distance (Avenue B, 1986)

Mobile/Mobile (Echo Park, 1987)

Rustic Diversions (Echo Park, 1988)

[where late the sweet] BIRDS SANG (O Books, 1989)

Sonnets (Potes & Poets, 1989)

Before Photography (THE Press, 1991)

Metalmorphosis (THE Press, 1991)

five (Slim Press, 1991)

Selected Letters (Zasterle, 1992)

spaces in the light said to be where one/ comes from (Potes & Poets, 1992)

PRIVATE (Leave Books, 1993)

Present Tense (The Figures, 1995)

Sculpture (Littoral Books, 1996)

Mallarmé: poem in prose (Santa Barbara Review Publications, 1998)

Idea's Mirror (Potes & Poets, 1999)

SOUND/ (system) (Green Integer, 2002)

Portraits & Repetition (The Post-Apollo Press, 2002)

REAL (Avenue B, 2007)

CLOUD / RIDGE (ubu editions, 2007)

HUMAN / NATURE (ubu editions, 2007)

CRITICISM

Campion: On Song (Routledge & Kegan Paul, 1981)

Listening to Reading (SUNY Press, 2000)

Reading the Unseen: (Offstage) Hamlet (Counterpath Press, 2010)

Conversation

Stephen Ratcliffe

Bootstrap Productions
2011

Some of these poems have appeared in the following:

Angle, Antenym, Columbia Poetry Review, First Intensity, Lingo, Mirage #4/Period(ical), New American Writing, Proliferation, Rhizome, Ribot, Salt, Situation, Talisman, Texture, Walrus, and *W/Edge.*

Cover art: Henri Matisse, Conversation, 1908-12.
Oil on canvas, 69 5/8 x 85 3/8 inches. Reprinted
with permission of The State Hermitage Museum,
St. Petersburg. Photograph © The State Hermitage Museum.

Bootstrap Productions
82 Wyman Street
Lowell, MA 01852

Plein Air Editions is an imprint of Bootstrap Productions,
Inc. a non-profit arts and literary collective founded by
Derek Fenner and Ryan Gallagher.

Plein Air Editions are curated and edited by Tyler Doherty
and Tom Morgan and designed by Charlie Laughtland.

ISBN-13: 978-0-9821600-6-0

Bootstrap Productions
bootstrapproductions.org
Distributed by Small Press Distribution

Conversation

how the voice is going forward in such a measure, conversation in whose scope the man is standing

facing her, as if what he wants to say will reach the porch of her left ear the moment she hears it,

where the telephone ringing at 7:20 will be the same person, the sound in the floor that isn't a bird

chipping on the roof, meaning that to repeat what 'you' has seen in such a place includes everything

except points on a scale called the hand that is holding yours, from which one will learn to desire the person in the blue shirt meaning one who thinks, being productive in the sense that one can read

books on a beach birds fly over making wind sounds, where the wind is blowing in a direction opposite

the other person at a different angle looking down or to her right or left depending on the position

of the observer who is driving the blue car forward, having spent time in the same place as someone

else ('you') who drives up from behind, pulls alongside, looks a couple of times before driving on the geometry of lines defined by the tangent of water and sand upon which shells have a limited life,

the passage from one person's eyes to the other's whose color changes depending on what is reflected,

grey of sky or the heather of low grasses whose tips scratch hieroglyphs into the dust of the path

one is walking after someone else, two deer positioned on the cracked brown water has evaporated

available thus to be walked on, the feet of the person making wine stained purple, crushed grapes

attracting hundreds of bees as if fermentation were feeling as much as pulp, skin, stems and seeds walking across a lawn (green) how one will be struck by peripheral vision, as if voices onstage

could reach up through the building through which heat rises, the man who staggers up the aisle

after the performance followed by the woman whose face registers what it means to face the end

of his life, counting that clock linked to the man in a hotel room who suddenly finds himself

alone with a gun, the one beside him having shot herself dead, that music as it enters the ear

of someone whose eyes will be closed, that person drifting backward or sideways from the person

on the balcony to the one ('you') who may be walking across a similar stretch of fresh-cut grass to get beyond what one wants, a road whose curves extend the perception of what may be thought

more than pleasing, articulate as bodies moving separately in the motion that precedes sleep,

eyes whose red suggests the measure of desire in someone who begins to forget the circumstance

he is moving through, thinking for instance of the bed in the room through whose windows (closed)

moonlight streams, the light turned down in whose twin pale scope one sees how abandoned the face

whose mouth gapes in the dark that goes on overhead becomes, measured as one imagines that graph

that pictures heat, the brush of body (kelp) or flesh of someone's lips the moment one bites it that room in fluorescent light after the voice stops, how the person at the other end of the line

sounds picking it up in the middle of a different conversation, man in blue pajamas facing someone

in a black robe who sits looking up at him not relaxed, the window between them in exactly the same

position as this one, beyond whose perimeter desire will continue to shine when the car drives away

the next morning, grey birds in the field lighting up when the front door opens, the man walks out

the next morning, grey birds in the field lighting up when the front door opens, the man walks out

meaning it is possible to do that, possible for the mouth to open around consonants or the vowels

whose sense will be more than likely to enact what happened physically, meaning in place of that how if the sprinklers don't come on the grass (lawn) will turn (color), meaning the robin who startles

at the sound of the person at the window when he opens it walking from one house to the other, the red

front door whose discontinuities include the sense of coming into a room of people one of whom knows

'you' is present, how the green of a person's shirt will be echoed by salt-water green at the corner

of a table, fingers at the small of that person's back who turns to walk down the hall of a building

whose inhabitants continue to be present as bodies in space, half notes descending in place of that to think of how that person enters the room, already occupied by others who have driven the same roads

(multiple) in other words, who called the driver out of bed that morning, the sense that such a shadow

can be cast by an object (person) whose identity isn't known, the verb to follow the sun whose gender

appears to shift depending on its position in the line about "fair," "unhappy shadow" and other words

for the anxiety of moving twice within months, leaving a message whose message may well never be read how to be continued is missing the person to whom it may be addressed, not having spoken in one sense

being deprived of the physics of the speech whose sound constitutes thinking, the person at the table

whose legs will be crossed or the possibility of finding such a place before it disappears at the end

of the next line, meaning the other person will be thinking of the absence a reader can only guess at

as what happened (palimpsest) moves to a climax without climax, space at that point dependent on that juniper or pine on a west-facing ridge the wind blows against being in that sense wind-swept, exposed

to feel what wretches feel for instance on a stage, having stopped for hours in the middle of the day

to compose the letters of someone else's name, the person who may not want 'you' to be present moving

forward as a train starts up again in the distance, a certain slant of sunlight on the wings of birds

whose patterns of activity appear to be random points on a scale whose notes rise as if amplified,

leaves at the end of a season (dried) sounded as wind (rustling) or the sign of such wind as music limited by waking to sunlight in a white room, indirect in the sense that low clouds (fog) will filter

particles of a substance that otherwise passes through one's body as a hand reaches through the chest

of the person who means to fall asleep, fingernails that continue to grow could be accidently broken,

intensity of wind coming off the surfaces of water in a similar (evening) light such that one leans

sideways to get out of it, someone having walked up to touch one's shoulder, the line folding back

on itself a form of saying that complicated by the sound of someone's voice (filmed) at that pitch as if an object (log) appears in a dream in place of its location, an original feeling the body (head)

changed when a bottle spills water in a person's mouth who thinks of doing that, paralyzed by sitting

in the car (blue) next to the car (green) meaning the person doesn't come back, thinking the painting

of such a landscape could be made to represent what is going on between them, other events unfolding

on a page whose dimensions haven't been set, how the repetition of 6 in the phrase .66666666 stands

in that sense for the fraction of a heartbeat one can be said to hear (accident) listening to that how after rain the season in other words changes, driving in the car along the coast after having left

someone who is reading in a car, gets up the next morning only to lie down again (reading) on a couch

that was a bed, the way creases in a shoulder may be taken as a sign that one has slept whether 'you'

is acknowledged or not, the taste of salt on that person's fingers (tongue) hours later, the grass

under the birdbath greener than elsewhere meaning it is spilled, that accident analogous to the car

in the left hand lane whose engine is on fire, its driver (passenger) walking in the next frame away how that is to say birds will be scolding, the one putting lotion on her legs meaning they are dry

who has fallen asleep in the light of the neighbor's front porch, having moved across the same room

because of that person, the red Moroccan chair a phrase in the book she reads whose type is too small

to be seen without glasses, how the sun the moment before it disappears looks (red) in a certain lens

or sky whose clouds appear like graphic images (grids) someone has scanned on a machine such as that,

how the person leaning back against that rock will look up at clouds that look (overhead) like that how the one driving away will be made to feel that way, having slept when the back goes into knots

(spasms) or shoulder aches after days of that, the mouth at another person's mouth making gestures

the body means as sense, beads of sweat on the belly of the person who is reading in a metal chair

or the impression of metal on skin at the small of the back 'you' sees turning accidently around,

how moisture collects at the mouth whose tongue will appear to be moving in such light forward,

another driving at the speed sound defines as motion minus the pull a shoulder makes lifting away walking away from the car whose windows are washed, the person who writes the message meaning to talk

to someone reading (mail) from elsewhere, clothes on a chair in front of a fire because one will step

from the shower directly into them, the cup that held coffee placed in the blue corner of the floor

by the passenger who feels what transpires when one wakes after leaning back in the chair (metal)

whose grid presses the small of her back, 'you' meaning that position occupied by one hemisphere's

response to its other half placed for example as the fit (wet) of two figures standing in that glass the man in the car whose window (open) appears to let his smoke evaporate, how orange signs at the side

of the road cause other cars to slow down, for example thinking about whether someone could be driving

back to the bank, the woman at the window whose skin (blistered) means she refuses to take your check

because she doesn't know the 'you' whose signature appears on the back of it, as if to read the letter

one wants to send to the house next door could make the man feel drawn, want to smoke again in the car

whose window (rolled down) lets his smoke escape, won't end up (smashed) in the fence next to that one so blue the sky behind leaves (falling) appears to be melting, the person who walks across the field

meaning to dry her hair in the sun whose warmth in such wind will be measured as the limit of desire,

as ice applied to the muscle (inflamed) will drive fluid elsewhere, certain drugs taken at intervals

to relax the body causing a person to fall into a sleep in which 'you' is having sex with the person

beside 'you,' a voice on the telephone knowing the listener has slept all night on the kitchen floor

unable to crawl from the scene of the crime, not that one moves into position on the following page meaning this one, the line at the top analogous in that position to an ice pack (wrapped) in place

in the crevice between the front of one thigh and the torso of the person who wants to walk forward,

on the next page of the story someone asleep between the other person's legs instead of driving away,

the sound one hears including a description of birds (unidentified) lifting from a thicket of grass

behind which deer walk, wind coming up in the middle of the night, muscles relaxed in the presence

of heat (moist) in conjunction with a drug whose name suggests how flexible one becomes doing that intervention being a form of swallowing the pill whose effects will be felt for hours, say that one

body falls asleep in that position (flat) or curled next to the person who wants to be told a story,

letters in a certain dimension (light) disappearing as 'you' says reading behind your back, turning

the hips in the opposite direction to where the arms (shoulders) mean to be set, the cast of light

as one walks from the door to the place where ice is being made, thus how it feels to be pressing

against that part of the leg whose muscles (spasm) want to be moving elsewhere, extended, relaxed the one who has stepped from the car (passenger) to the one parked all night in that lot, walking up

to the door later in other clothes having talked to others, writing in a letter something about how

what is happening to 'you' changes as that name shifts on paper (accident), how the play one reads

might be performed on a stage by the person who sings instead of speaks her lines, a man at the door

whose part will include moving leaves from one place to another as air moves, voices at such a pitch

loud enough to be heard above the measure whose instruments converge in unison exactly at that point or say that in waking one can't move without that heat applied to the leg, the problem in that case

being to adjust whatever leaves the line last mentioned alone, returning at night to the building

(locked) understood as reading left to right or top to bottom (matrix) based on whether one has

received the letter or not, chooses not to respond not because 'you' has appeared at the door

(heartbeat) between the person's sense of himself and himself, how one position is continuous

as the sound of two syllables (shifting) position in the area mapped as someone's bed, nerves

press down in any case (kneecap) once the leg is pulled, stretched or otherwise made to relax the person in bed meaning to relax, taking off one's clothes in the middle of the day (afternoon)

having been dressed in the backyard, how dozens of birds can lift as 'you' passes the canvas chair

when the telephone rings, landing on the ground when a person walks up (camouflaged) whose left leg

falls asleep, as if going upstairs to lie down instead of sitting in the yellow chair (metal) might

photograph the person at the window looking out, the second person ('you') singular whose leg wakes

(numb) meaning that he wants to walk around and later appears to be sitting by the window, watching as if staying in that position (prone) so many hours could make the body assume its own image, the one

'you' becomes getting out of bed without speaking, knowing that something has happened offstage (play)

therefore not exactly present for the person watching that scene, as a landscape (room) can be entered

by someone walking toward the person who stands in the kitchen making coffee, a connection (internal)

spoken of in terms of a plot whose dimensions will change depending on the page she happens to open,

orchids in the morning light (outside) for instance opposite an orchid on the table in the window outside, the landscape of clouds at dawn lit from a source the person at the window sees only later,

as if the future could be present as a listing of the objects arranged on a table or hung between

the vertical windows on a wall, still lifes of glasses (empty) whose surfaces reflect a pale violet

illusion of cloth behind them, a tableau of quince spilling out of a bowl (turned) next to the corner

'you' walks into on photographic paper, the person whose sight (peripheral) seems otherwise to shrink

or frame itself (glass) as the inside figure whose thinking can thus be said to approximate her face the face that wakes (drawn) having walked into a yard in which birds appear in positions, the person

insisting that the view of a landscape articulates what is happening (foreground) by drawing the eye

back and to the left, following a road or line of buildings (roofs) from bottom right to top (sky)

behind the plane of a mountain whose summit is a part of the whole, the landscape of a sentence

in that case an arrangement of words in the phrase (prepositional) 'you' appears to be thinking,

the sound of twelve o'clock inaccurate in the sense that someone can only pretend to be different

arriving by telephone (message), whose name begins with an incomplete thought one means to continue that a voice could catch the emotion 'you' feels in such a position, as if suspended above the other

one is about to commit an act whose consequences will go on a long time, the configuration of objects

placed on the wall of the front room reflective of certain past events (composed) meaning to be taken

in that order, how the vase can be filled with water and the vine some of whose flowers have bloomed,

behind which the wing of a bird (sculpture) gives way to person on a wave for whom water is a motion

of the body contained in what moves through it, be that fluid or the impulse (nerve) that attends it how weather changes what takes place in it, the feeling one has waking up to the sound not of water

exactly but a south wind blowing in the branches of trees in the first place, speaking of how letters

in the last word of a line ("grow") disappear in the sense that meaning may be talked about in terms

of that expression, the person's face 'you' will suggest turning over in bed, pulling up the blanket

or sitting in a chair downstairs in front of the fire some of whose wood will be wet, the frog (green)

translated as a series of black and white photographs (visual) whose long grey scale is its signature instead of reading which words, one hears what it is to make the sound of strings (plucked) measure

the scale a voice follows after a while, say 'you' wakes in a line whose apparent direction changes

the conversation between someone driving (rain) and how the other person will look sitting on a bench

in the shade of that building, speaking of the man in the dream whose shoulders fill his shirt (green)

positioned in a visual line, how what is missing from this description follows a shape backward from

the left to the shape of the mountain (geometric) white as the sky that surrounds it, words the way

that person (conscious) comes after the fact that one happens to be listening to the sound of that call it weather, the way one thinks of the person (named) as component parts, a confusion of trees

meaning hair or lawn or kind of cloth 'you' shows up wearing over the shoulder (green) in a picture

(first) the photographer's thumb registered as a detail in the foreground, behind which the reader's

face disappears, how the light will appear to someone who thinks what is happening in the other words

(different) extended on a map whose order of things continues to be thought approximate to that chair

beside the fire, that car stopped on the bridge in a wind or the way branches can be blowing inside

sleep, as if what is being remembered minus the shape it takes folded as a fabric (shirt) or face turned to face the other person, who sits in a blue chair on the other side of the window (open)

facing the park, lawn, tree and the neighbor's window (closed) in which he may be reading, the bird

who flirts when 'you' walks across the yard in a straight line (extended) to get another piece of wood

or leave in the car (blue) that morning, how it was driving without being able to stop, park or drink

a glass even of water, picture gliding under the lip of the wave (green) on the wall beside a window

to another view, where the person instead of standing (profile) looking directly at 'you' whose arm

appears to be indistinguishable from the railing whose letters seem to spell "now" is looking out the same window (open) the next morning because it is warmer, a close-up of hands on the wheel driving

'you' (missing) in a line about the airport from which one has departed, the other picture of someone

who is driven looking down or to the side meaning to avoid the camera (focus) metaphorically that is,

that idea analogous to standing (profile) in a view framed by a rectangle the color of which (blue)

the wall makes apparent as rhythm or the sound of cars passing the fence, beyond which one thinks

what it means to look back at the window whose curtain is pulled back, the character in the novel

who bites his finger (index) or washes his hands before crawling down under the blankets to sleep all night without waking, the one who has taken her seat in the blue chair looking up at the person

whose arm is bent, his hand in his pocket meaning to identify something about the character (novel)

named after what he does with his hand (thumb) as a memory of that, how the telephone isn't the same

as the one who calls 'you' (pronoun) in other words former, her shape in that sense the sound it makes

in a line about the ear (foreground) parallel to the coastline one sees in the distance driving away

from it, wind in the other direction not in place of that phenomenon (telephone) but moving beyond

feeling what has happened will continue as long as she thinks he is talking (separate) about that the one at the window looking out of the picture too far away to be seen, buoyed up on a curtain

(missing) the wind blows in after a storm, having gone out for a walk meaning only to get some air

'you' settles in a line the sidewalk follows on the way to a room whose chairs will be full, the man

who continues to speak without recognition of his place in the culture of that place (body) of chairs

as if to say again what it will be to look across the blue frame of the window directly at the person

facing the microphone, the form of whose hands may or may not be seen as a turn in the conversation

whose next passage will appear to be moving closer (decoy) to what it is exactly she means to add picking up the phone in that tone of voice, having been interrupted by what she doesn't say directly

(abrupt) on that subject, as if to tell the person one has called someone (elsewhere) to determine

what is going on will make 'you' appear to the reader who opens her book to an argument whose logic

isn't a surprise, the audience in that case not the woman to whom he addresses himself but other men

(unseen) who may be taken to have read him, 'you' thus posited as someone who is driving that morning

after such a conversation (unplanned) has happened, the rehearsal of such events meaning not to play

them out beforehand but close that scene, begin what is about to unfold parallel to that distortion at the beginning of the story whose characters will continue to talk at cross purposes, as 'you'

remembers the next frame (titled) like a chair whose body hasn't arrived, the reason she is going

forward on that subject a matter of what the other person does to her more than design (unconscious),

birds still about to be seen in the part about the person who is standing (profile) facing the person

whose arm rests on the arm of the chair, the house divided into pictures whose value includes emotion

as much as distance (negotiable) or the sound a person makes moving away, a window in the background

an echo of the one 'you' looks through watching them talk, that conversation equal to being (quote) without necessarily showing it, how the man can pick up the phone meaning to call someone so far away

the next day has started, that connection (heat) allowing what has happened to be spoken of in terms

of weather (rain) or the temperature in the room when one sits in front of the fire reading a book,

the dream about the person who returns to a former house, waits for the others to leave by walking

out the gate, 'you' becoming the person one is driving to meet in the line about cars on the freeway

whose lights have been turned on (anonymous), a signal meaning not that she isn't waiting to be called

(child) but hasn't yet begun to speak in a voice that sounds like someone else's (unknown), who leaves in person, having been at the center of that group of people to whom one feels something tangible

(color) as the sound of a voice ascending half a tone behind the beat, the one on the left making

'you' leave a circle of conversation within which someone appears as the background of that place,

abstract in the sense that the blue lines (bars) extend horizontally across the top of the picture

as a person who speaks registers forms of irritation one chooses not to repeat, certain instruments

missing the beat, the direction one is then going not simply abstract (sunlight) but felt in the way

leaves look turning on the tree, fallen to the sidewalk where 'you' walks thinking (words) about that or how when the telephone rings the person isn't there, 'you' in that case so far away the speaker

finishes what he thinks (question) before it registers that sound, meaning to go out in the street

will invite gestures, what is meant by rubbing up against the crotch of the female in that culture

equal to being alone in that place (telephone) where one is calling back, not reaching the person

whose letter is addressed to three names one of whom appears to be 'you' in the second position,

as if in moving the chair to that corner of the yard (sun) one might finish the letter to someone

whose postcard appears to be without feeling, that sense (inaccurate) being converged [sic] by hand according to music itself, whose rhythms may be taken to register the presence of feeling the body

knows when 'you' picks up the phone, the sound of that person's voice when what is going on (inside)

becomes visible (angle) as an acoustic shape in that sense, danger for instance walking down a street

out of which men will appear to press themselves against her body, go away into the dark only to come

back again (assault) again without restraint, that malaria itself will be known as a possible danger

in places like that (island) far from what one thinks will be happening next, the descent of notes

played by hand (strings) meaning to be heard (understood) as a text in place (elsewhere) of that at the bottom of the hill the place one thinks was a home, meaning the other person turns on the light

or walks down the hall from one room (white) to the next, the person asleep (alone) in a cast-iron bed

(single) who wakes up in front of the fireplace (embers) by whose light words can be written, that man

on the radio having been shot singing (sound) "stand by me" (as if it were possible), the woman blamed

(narrative) having told him to go away, his being in a chair by the fire when the lights come back on,

the phone machine's clicks recording that fact, the image of the flame going out or feeling of hair

one is touching at the back of his neck (curls) when the man on the guitar (acoustic) starts over the sound of the voice (reading) what he thinks, that one will be the subject of such a set of lines

organized in a three-dimensional space (room) in which people stop talking when the telephone rings,

someone who is reading by extension (continuous) of herself in air, the parts of a body anatomized

as if in pieces its effect upon those who observe it may be determined as sound or the echo sound

makes entering the ear, imaginary in that what the other person understands by a gesture (apology)

isn't reflected by her actions in the next scene, someone no longer wanting to talk with the person

moving to a chair at the edge of a room in which others may be sitting, listening to that being read at that time (morning) meaning light will be coming through the cloud or leaves of the tree (green)

as if to be separated by such a space is the definition 'you' will suggest in that line of thought,

the distance between the one at the table in a window and what he sees in that light (green) or hears

when the other person's tongue begins to approach meaning to be doing that (interrupted) in the dark,

the room itself in place of what happens later in a different conversation, the man no longer standing

opposite the one in the blue chair facing him (window) but placed in the yard where birds will be seen

flitting up to bushes or down again, 'you' in that case meaning to be asleep because of taking that up by hand as words in the mouth mean to articulate that feeling (asleep) the person turns aside, dreams

of how one will appear on the front steps of the former house (white) having returned from that place

a letter interrupts by the rhythm of the same words repeated without stopping, the instrument meaning

the line about to be taken up in the next score (polyphonic) whose materials include birds scratching

out the window beside which the neighbor's house will be built, his hand in the pocket of his pajamas

(blue) extended at an angle equal to how far her knee bends in such a case, her appearance understood

at this point to represent the person who is starting to explode in anger, "who do you think you are" to which there isn't an answer, the person who wakes 'you' at the end of the dream in which the table

will be piled with papers and books, the rain outside lifting to the point that one sees the contours

of the ridge (clouded) whose trees will have been cut, a snapshot in the upstairs bedroom whose walls

haven't yet been painted (white) looking out the window viewed as an act of perception minus distance

beyond which the same landscape will be only a concept, the woman meaning in that sense to be someone

'you' designates on the page about the person who is reading her position in a line, the idea of such

a photograph of the girl on the beach being that she is smiling, hand positioned on his left shoulder when one sees the ridge clouds lift to expose, a conversation whose direction will be pointed out

meaning to make sense of what has taken place in the history 'you' begins to write in other words

(structure) sitting in a chair, the cigarette for instance in the left hand next to music one hears

after the dream about being in the room whose ceiling has been replaced with acoustic tile, the person

whose shape changes (mother) when she turns to address the audience, the animal whose part was removed

(surgery) in order to extend the direction one walks (right) on the way to the airport with two bags,

one of which contains a theory of prose wrapped in a blue towel which may be something to sleep on flying overhead, as clouds may be said to rise on a curtain of air the heat at such latitudes lifts

higher than the plane, whose language begins to be recognized as the object one is thinking (image)

standing at the desk because the others haven't arrived, the boy with the knife in his pocket made

to take it out before he passes into the next room (device) on his way to another mode of thinking,

the telephone having interrupted the dream about the man who seems to forget the placement of objects

in a magazine whose pictures will be described in another language, that person feeling less driven

to call 'you' the second person on the phone (blue) meaning the water will be warmer, more buoyant caught in the flashlight for instance walking downstairs from a room whose walls are missing, ceiling

constructed of materials one turns up in the theory of prose whose word for the most ordinary of acts

(sleep) becomes a challenge, the man in the hat whose child answers the phone in a different language

driving a truck whose plates aren't legal, the fan on the ceiling whose function is to circulate air

(humid) in a room whose windows are open (missing) because it is hot, the girl who goes to the dance

meaning the second person ('you') doesn't go, the boy whose hair (blond) reminds her of her sister's or sound of mariachis on the tape that doesn't stop, the man asking for someone to walk to the store

like an object in the culture of a place (music) where the sun comes up out of palm trees on a beach,

the feeling water has pushing through it for instance turning under the silver-edged lip of the wave

the wind holds up, being pulled off the land because heat rises (moisture), 'you' having no definition

like someone who wakes up before first light dreaming of someone who continues to stand at the window,

hand in a pale blue pocket meaning he faces the woman (seated) he hasn't even called to say he's left another country, as if place could be written in terms of the word for table, the person 'you' called

an actor (television) walking through the poorest part of town, the building on the corner (turquoise)

where the dog sleeps or bus stops on its way to the plot whose direction (alternative) includes a boat

pulled up on the sand whose engine has stopped, the man who has assaulted other people and a boy prior

to appearing in a doorway (dark) driving the same truck forward, speaking of what it means to practice

nouns for objects on the table or the sound of animals waking up from sleep hours before or after that line moving forward to a building that isn't a film or book in another language but the same thing

meaning to be in that place, 'you' for instance in the line leveled by two men in sandals and hats,

the silver that frames each tooth of the first one (maestro) in the form the wave takes as it builds

outside to the left in a description of the sun coming up behind palm trees at the edge of the beach

analogous to the name of the foreign country, something itself beside or in front of another (voices)

voices subtract, a text on the facing page (stencil) of a world that precedes or otherwise covers it represented as feeling (alarm) walking down a road in the dark where people stand without speaking,

whether the man was killed last night and where he lies across the street the girl whispers (scared)

in broken Spanish, the logic of such a picture correct except why was her brother walking with a gun

if the bandit was still in the house, undertones in the foreground beyond which animals will be heard

as an image (outside) of this place, possible in the sense that 'you' exists in relation to the object

(present) expressed in terms of one's incomplete knowledge of what has actually happened (and to whom) assuming it wasn't a story, say that the man who was walking now lay dead in a ditch across a road,

one bullet hole in his stomach and one in the chest where the boy had meant to shoot him (Fernando)

walking back across the road to work, that person opposed to another in whose symbolic notation 'you'

(verbal) is a concept of someone other than the one asking if things are that simple, meaning the word

for "salt" might be the answer to the question the other boy will ask in a different series (negative)

typical of that place, the story for instance of the person who likes to spend time reading in a chair under a tile roof, the view from the table including those who are about to enter the water minus

their child, the dog who will not grow up to bark all night (neighbors) according to a single plan,

the proposition that 'you' can move to a foreign country without missing a beat by means of objects

(things) at the end of the next sentence, the logic of that picture complicated by the fact that one

can lose track of the surface upon which a description of the motion of water (flat) will be written,

how someone may think after days in that place that what has happened will seem to turn not on how

one wants it but the mistakes someone has made meaning (otherwise) to do something other than that set of options, returning to find that person asleep in the other person's bed (intentional) meaning

to wake 'you' attached on a note to the door, the way a bird soars above cliffs as the wind lifts it

("found") for that reason, lights in the window a frame for what could be contained when the subject

(isolated) calls on the telephone a minute after one thinks of him watching 'you' pick up the phone,

abstract in the sense that the letter explains how the woman doesn't want to be called or talked to,

turning when 'you' speaks to address her counterpart's claim that it isn't the fact of such an object

but the wave's size in proportion to the distance it travels multiplied by its motion (mutual) squared assuming the bed can be moved somewhere else, picture a situation logic describes by driving on a road

("hypothetical"), how it is that one can be talking on the phone to someone whose package has arrived,

wanting to let that person know the function of an object (tree) transformed by the position of lights

or sounds in the room, this phenomenon clear in the sense that a reader assumes she doesn't understand

what 'you' intends to argue (character) repeated in another direction, someone under the covers moving

to his left in order to experience the possibility that a prior event can be repeated as another thing

(involved) say in a different room, that thing in relation to an individual without whom one will stop

—

thinking of that, the dog who follows meaning to be close to what cannot be expressed as an ending,

prefix, changes in the object 'you' becomes going out the door (conclusive) or answering the phone

according to rules whose logic is purely mathematical, the pull of the muscle in one person's back

assumed to articulate (question) what the child wants across the room, as if things could be called

watching 'you' speak as a description in place of that picture, the dog whose tongue is out (gesture)

not meaning to be restrained between the object of his desire and the proposition that image exists

(represented) in the form of the person one means in comparison to something that is yet to appear

speakers set to convey the sound the man makes (camera) simultaneously to that, how a series of rocks

can be carried from one place to another by means of a complex of structures whose values (aesthetic)

include the woman who doesn't want to see 'you' filmed in deep water, those two characters standing

relative to the child who has disappeared on the one hand (ambiguous) on a plane in the second chapter

before this one, the rock falling on the other (nothing) instead of thinking she has changed her mind,

the orchestra at that point taking over (volume) for the man who otherwise would be speaking of this speaking of the film in which blood is made (picture) to spill against the glass or car or man's face

who is driving, rocks in the back seat adding more weight than one had driving the opposite direction

to 'you' (arrived) meaning in the second car, how it is that the method of physics reaches the object

connected by its function in the relationship (negative) next to the one who appears in the same line

understood to be someone other than her child, accepting that proposition as a term below the surface

(stone) of a building whose other stones may also be driven or placed in the yard one may walk across

in a direction relative to this one, the fact that 'you' is looking at pictures (possibly) of figures where 'you' appears to be thinking of something else, which isn't possible given the angle of the sun

above the horizon (noon) or the sound of a bird feeding in some given place, as if what is being said

by the person "A" who sits in her chair to the right of the window were a simple thing (object) heard

as a voice from the neighbor's house, the function of the person sleeping in that logic <u>not</u> concerned

with the position of the other's arm on her chair (blue) or the absence of her feet in the foreground,

the sentence going on about the man who was killed having flown to that place knowing what it means

(grammar) to say for example that one word refers to another in the sense that 'you' are thinking the man whose work isn't work, listening to others talk about how what happened (has) happened the way

description on that level made it possible, the animal whose head appears at the edge of a hole (dirt)

beside the person who decides to stop because her hands are shaking, as logic will propose to situate

the house in order to maximize its exposure to the sun, the shortest days of winter at that latitude

meaning 'you' is the object of a preposition whose function means to be false, the woman's position

on top of the man (chair) equal to falling asleep in somebody's else's bed, his leg kicked over hers

when she turns aside to determine the name of objects complicated by their place in the next sentence after thinking it, the man (speaking) who finds himself on a dark street about to be given photographs

equivalent to the person standing in a foreign country, how something takes care of itself (structure)

described as the motion of a bird positioned above its unseen prey, 'you' in that statement changing

in relation to an object that is itself connected for instance to the figure standing like a column

(blue) against the blue field of the wall, this operation as "method" of points in a scale (visual)

whose composite parts regress to a distance (space) in which each object appears to follow itself,

two shadows in the picture on the left being cast in a negative sense (mechanical) because of that the view from an upstairs window, how dogs will be seen first where the animal was (disappeared)

then walking into the background, the bird whose wings kept it stationary in the middle distance

perched (binoculars) in a different line (green) written as the negative, which isn't to say how

the man thinks can be expressed as a proposition included in what 'you' mean turning over in bed

(domestic) or turning out the light prior to falling asleep, the interval between the experience

of walking toward the ocean (distant) after the sun has dipped into clouds as opposed to waiting

and that person speaking, believing whatever is meant by her silence will admit that she is gone in the work about form, content no longer being what takes place between the person driving (north)

and what he thinks, how simple to say confusion brings 'you' to this place when in fact the other

person isn't responsible for the feelings she has or image she continues to hold of him, idealism

of the body that is itself a projection of what he believes to have been the case or rather keeps

wanting, as if desire also belongs on the side that chooses to see what happens in terms (visual)

parallel to one's idea of the world as a different form (fact) of the concept "and so on," example

of knowing exactly who he is or what to do or what it means to say nothing except what can be said aside from the painting on the wall, whose subject (orange) isn't analogous to the color or shape

of chrome yellow in relation to alizarin crimson that goes toward red, the glaze he applies (amber)

after 'you' leaves to see the woman who plans to extract a tooth (left) meaning by that act to remove

a tendency toward infection, given the object one sees as its surfaces exists in reference to an idea

she continues to appear in place of, the car (green) parked in front of a house, as a picture is said

to approximate the subject it describes by means of pigment or shade, flake white or sap green (glaze)

standing for the weight of the lemon which isn't that at all, this view of the interior from the left amounting to a portrait of the person himself, driving across the valley toward a piling up of clouds

in front of which birds are lifting away from 'you' (asymmetrical), one relaxes having left the house

as in a proposition one can see a landscape by looking to the side, that view more than meets the eye

because it isn't a complete picture of someone waking up, the man who wants to leave the woman feeling

(closer) meaning in the smallest of gestures, the object in the foreground (orange) which is floating

in an endless sea of black paint that may or may not appear glazed given the temperature in the room in relation to the temperature outside, weather at that latitude a factor in how (elevation)

a person feels changing his clothes, having come to this place by means of the body's fatigue

moving up hill into a landscape the painter himself has given up, the object in the foreground

(orange) between its present shadow and the perception of the sound it makes against the place

in the road (clearing) one decides to stop, the second person 'you' means to remember thinking

in a different (previous) scene in which the person who arrives (father) seems to be crawling

into a sleeping bag, watching how steam from three warm bodies is pumping out into the night meaning to keep going, someone in front kicking steps in the snow (awake) as if that were the only way

forward in a logic one is given to speak in sentences whose object (grammar) continues to be absorbed,

the distance between one's senses where 'you' is the subject of the picture he sees closing his eyes,

roses or tulips or a lemon for instance standing in a light that is internal to the painting itself,

which might easily be understood as a self-portrait of that person (abstract) even though he appears

not to be present, a sound of wind in trees above them suggested in place of snow (visible) piling up layer upon layer, meaning to turn down hill before dark (tracks) having stayed too long in the snow,

how the person who is moving into that landscape (divide) thinks about where to take the next step

(left) or how 'you' will be getting on the airplane elsewhere, another chapter having been closed

no matter how often the man thinks to himself about the way she arranged the furniture in a room

or looked in a picture taken in a foreign city with the child on a bench looking down, her white

dress standing both for that time of year (summer) and her age (eight) at the time of that event,

knowing that what has happened is as much a matter of action as anything another person has done to have changed it, not falling asleep under trees (tent) because the wind would come in gusts

approaching the sound of snow being blown, as if one were present in the picture of those three

for instance on the deck of a boat as the sun rose (Mediterranean) instead of such a place, cold

and desolate as the absence of its road (disappeared) under snow, looking back in that direction

at a barren stretch of flat (light) between the hill and mountain one has left, how 'you' enters

the first person singular (grammar) whose logic calls for getting on a plane, a man of few words

being asked a series of questions about the habitat (windblown) or condition (swept) of the road above the house, the ridge across which wind was clocked at 128 miles an hour (reported) the day 'you'

started back, sound of snow falling from trees under which three men appeared to be sleeping, the one

in the middle dreaming of another person (S) about whom one's fears may be said to surface, that form

of action (adventure) including the way he drives in a car or walks ahead of 'you' (implied) meaning

not to injure his leg, returning by that means across the state whose fields are flooded (landscape)

on a road strewn with debris (green) torn from trees by such wind, this description being inadequate

to register what has taken place in the sound for example of wind or fact that one is given a letter from 'you,' being in that case in a foreign country (I) whose language includes words for cloth, music

and the way rain falls from clouds on the horizon (blue) weather changes when the front passes through,

how the plane itself can lift through that condition without disturbance given its range of possible

dimensions on a scale from one to nine objects, one of which is the size of its handwriting measured

against the page 'you' appears to be thinking, reader therefore unable to sleep because the relation

of future events to what has happened elsewhere (film) in the room where the girl is running obliquely

away from the camera (three) continues to be adjusted, a form never less than attention to its content the way the sky (cloud) clears as the land heats up, the water turns blue reflecting the form (dome)

say of an island whose mountain, measured from the floor of that body (arithmetic) means to be taken

as the position of the observer hears it spoken, the one who wakes to where the fire swept buildings

(disappeared) or names of objects or places in an alphabet in which letters have been lost (missing),

this thought for instance expressed by the consonants h, k, l, m, n, p, and w in various combinations

with the vowels a and so on, a point 'you' (name) insists will be registered in the distance as water

breaks at the mouth of the harbor, the doctor who gets up at night to heat more liquid for his throat two days prior to this, how many different people walking without shoes over fields of lava (cooled)

in heat, whether in summer as the high moves north (stationary) or after the year turns, clouds move

down from the mountain one sees as a dome (flat) from which it issued, leave signs of their presence

etched in stone, rocks 'you' may be said to place on the edge of a person's body who has fallen back

on the sand, the grammar of his sentence held up for all to see in the dream at the end of that mind,

the fact that a well can be drilled at the center of a conversation that seems to continue the sound

in words of the man whose hearing (connected) imagines what it means to refer to this chain of events including wind, which the man with a telephoto lens at the edge of water (coral) says is coming,

say that 'you' drapes parts of her body over the leg of the person whose meaning is to be action

this way, driving south to the place where one rides waves longer than this position abbreviated

(A), the sound of the forest in relation to water independent of each other (recorded) as a form

of weather may be said to shift from one conversation (picture) to the next, one whose tendency

to speak of certain things (smoke) in one situation might appear to change the subject ('you')

to what one thinks of his former friend, child, dog, the projection of waves on another island or direction of the swell when it comes up, how the first clouds to catch the sun's light on another

side of the mountain (volcano) continue to change in reference to this, description a limit extended

from the object to someone still asleep in bed (breath) named 'you,' her method of finding the piece

(missing) subject to asking someone else to stand at a table in a corner of the room instead of that,

meaning its name will be spelled in a way not equivalent to how it will be spoken by the man driving

in a truck (blue) who wants to be described in a phrase whose object (water) keeps moving, this fact

of wind placed in the landscape chosen for its potential to remain a project that will never be done why one is there (island) overlooking the sea, into which the sun appears to flash (green) setting

events including a series of holes in the horizontal surface of the picture (landscape) like zero

in arithmetic, a tree watered in a circle whose function that person says follows its form, color

of dirt not washing away hours after he has finished moving rocks, a green that isn't part of what

he wants (desire) after 'you' disappears from the same sentence whose grammar represents this event,

the surface of the table for example covered with pieces of a picture whose shapes (random) could be

defined as the distance between two (surfaces), the other person sitting at that point next to 'you' no further away than the bird outside the window, after scratching at something on the roof (sounds)

making its call to one in a tree, the person in bed who hears this having arrived in that situation

from a different logical place (image) described by holding still, feeling in the sense of analysis

or direction of objects 'you' represents (parts) in a series of thoughts including this, the person

meaning to say for example that the form of an object will change when he carries it into the house

(closed) that hasn't been lived in for a week, its floor buckled because the ceiling leaks (picture)

a possible substitute for the view from a hammock on the porch, looking out at that expanse of blue facing west (Friday) in another climate, a chair the wind has blown into the canyon below the house

(square) whose view includes water, the sound of such wind coming down from the mountain (volcano)

covered by clouds or the person still asleep in the bed, speaking of what it means in this place

when the inside of the window appears to be wet (identical) and the road closed by a similar logic,

'you' in this case the figure on a page in which wind in the same location is blowing in from water

(direct) as action leads to its consequence, the telephone for example waking the person (arbitrary)

after he has fallen back asleep thinking of an earlier dream about a position concerned with theory in which one reads a line listening and talking at the same time, the person who wakes up like that

(object) after having asked the body to be touched, that feeling in the small of her back (or hand)

that someone has twisted (blood) in another situation complicated by boxes on the floor for example,

a suitcase filled with books she hasn't read a figure of speech subject to analysis (contradiction)

'you' implies in the singular, as a point in a line about what someone (child) thinks is happening

on the next page, her eyes closed as the camera clicks in a snapshot taken in the foreign country

(I) one hasn't seen except in pictures, legs pulled apart in a movement (spoken) standing for "X" meaning one wakes, light at first reflected on a wall (white) that has been painted by a different man

conscious of this, the picture of an orange floating in what appears to be a world of black (contrast)

above the table which doesn't exist in relation to that object for example, as 'you' in the sentence

"the world I found" implies that the man standing to the left of the window has already walked away,

the person he was facing (seated) in a blue chair that isn't described except in relation to a wall

whose arms are resting on it (limit) because she hasn't moved, the picture of the child in a doorway

at one age (surface) or another when she turns to go out dressed as opposed to coming back on a plane unable to sleep, preceded by waking from a chapter about the glass of wine in Shakespeare (fiction)

the person who is asked supposes it will be called, the object of this thought "A" being resolved

when it is analyzed for instance in a picture of that person sitting at the wheel of a boat (child)

the ocean behind him tilts to his right, attention in that case focused on the way something happens

instead of being objective about what is going on now (image), 'you' then equal to a different person

driving with a headache because the road keeps following the contours of the mountain even (possible)

when it slides, in which case the picture means to make "sense" of pulling up the covers for a nap given that one hasn't slept, the second orchid on the floor below the window subject to when someone

decides to move (pressure) to another location, that image visible by means of film in water (fixed)

whose negative has apparently been lost, meaning that the person turning in the pocket of the wave

will not be enlarged by this description, 'you' not equivalent to moving boxes of assorted books

according to the structure of a sentence whose logics (scales) may be opposed, a note that sounds

the daughter's arrival from a foreign country on the one hand (map) a form of assertion on another,

one whose theory includes those two poles appearing to say nothing (contradiction) in place of that misunderstanding, the one who called wanting to talk (unidentified) causing the other to be hurt,

the key word (spoken) capable of being taken in another sense by the person who wakes up thinking

of his relation to (A) and (B) in terms of that logic, obvious in the way that a bird flies across

an open window (theory) as if one is made to do that and thus isn't able to change, these characters

based for instance on real people (pictures) whose names "outside" will be evident at that point (P)

whose negative she expresses by turning away, reading the paper (horoscope) a possible description

of what happens when 'you' follows the pattern (expressed) in which matches are piled up in a bowl as a form of sculpture, rocks placed one on top of the other (meditation) in a landscape that isn't

under water, this proposition then followed by the person for whom it will be painful to hear 'you'

on the phone asking about the second object (jigsaw) with a meaningless name, as if it were a thing

simply to be called by the person whose work has been interrupted by that conversation which (picture)

doesn't include the series of smaller rocks piled on the windowsill (counter-meditation) or the place

of the person in a foreign country (exact) about to get on a plane, this hypothesis to be tested only

when she calls from outside the picture to the left of this one, the bird heading into (morning) wind or perched (motionless) on a rock, the sculpture placed in that position as a simple object (thought)

may be analyzed in relation to what she doesn't say when the other person leaves the room, how water

may be standing for instance under the house without being heard (definition) parallel to the person

in the film who has lost his hearing in the sense (picture) that notes will be made to stand for what

he thinks, the one who isn't on the plane he tells 'you' as part of an incomplete fact whose structure

(fixed) includes the possibility that water could be running across the road or standing in the ditch

beside it, 'you' in that case meaning to arrive on a different plane (composed) photographed on a bed in a snapshot on the windowsill taken by the mother, which involves her in wanting to locate that

(knowledge) named in the letter 'you' will receive second-hand, the person in the blue chair (arms)

looking at the man on the opposite side of the window who doesn't speak, the picture (conversation)

not including that, by which one means to acknowledge the object in a definite sense of her feeling

about the person she faces divided by what has happened prior to this event, the sound for instance

of frogs in the field before so many days of rain made it "exist" (possible) or prior to that sound

the sound of water at the window, the one who appears (awake) reading selected letters in the dark one also waking up, having heard from the father that one has arrived from a foreign country (object)

when the person who might have spoken of this refuses to do so, that conversation replaced by the one

'you' means to remember in its original sense (open) divided into sections, one about the car driving

without lights (visual) following the logic by which one will make a list of everything in the house

including the picture that is a sign by itself, objects theoretical in the sense that books (complex)

may be taken out of the chest or pictures down from the wall in relation to the person who made them,

the sound for example of cars out the window (possible) in letters that seem to presuppose that fact or pictures (wrapped) positioned as if someone will see them, the distance between what is going on

in another house (white) and its description following at many points the motion of a play (Socrates)

some of whose action doesn't appear, the person who is called learning for instance that 'you' wanted

(prefix) to see him, certain classes of objects listed according to whether they are desired ("watch")

by the person who has moved away or rather been moved, the one who doesn't want to be called meaning

in terms of physics to continue the emotion imagined by the woman in the blue chair who doesn't speak,

as if a logical notation could express what is going on inside (simple) the person who is growing thin not wanting to eat, her skin (face) closer to the structure of bone than when she left (important)

the book on the table, 'you' in that case not knowing whether it is possible to be seen in the room

(picture) or whether he wants to be left alone, a physics for instance of the object in the sentence

"do you have anything else to tell me?" where 'you' is in the chair by the fire and "anything" known,

the body of the person who asks it material in the sense that she is looking away, how the bracelet

whose clasp is stamped with the name of the foreign country that isn't the place it came from (M)

stands for the distance between these two points, each person feeling it (verb) in relation to that nostalgia for what is past, examples of which are represented by the person who was missing (physics)

from this equation, isn't awake when 'you' (projected) meaning the person in the blue chair answers

continuing a function of wanting to do that in a material sense, how the sound of birds (structure)

on the telephone line fills the air (co-ordinates) meaning the picture is complicated by her return,

the form of the question "what do you think about 'A'" extended to the table in the room she sits in

talking to that person, that conversation (internal) meaning to construct the object of one's desire

(variable) analogous to simply talking in the afternoon or walking with that one (awake) in the dark across the flooded mesa, how many houses become examples of water (number) standing at ground level,

the person who has lost weight (legs) in clothes represented by a series of adjacent crayon patches

none of which contradicts the illusion she is happy, her reluctance to speak a function of distance

between her fingers for instance (yellow) and that place whose visual field has already disappeared,

impossible to describe (affect) listening to another language, 'you' in a sense turning over in bed

because the shade that keeps daylight out allows it to continue (object) to the picture of the woman

looking out from the door, telling him the other person (named) will be out before she shuts it again only to appear again in the next line (series) waking from a dream about moisture in the room, two

meaning what happens involves the illusion of phenomena, 'you' in a play where the wall is connected

to what the man says (physical) about that kind of person, how she sits in a chair in the conversation

that isn't taking place in a certain sense (complete) dependent on its visual field, the sound of cars

outside the window analogous to a tree or other window she is facing before she sees him (equilibrium)

thinking of what it means to be thinking that (revised), the letter for instance whose sum is a form

of bending taken as an object explained on the next page by someone who is thinking of someone else waking up from the dream about making a movie, line-up of people who will play the victims (chained)

one of whom is 'you' (thinking) behind the wheel of the truck, someone on the telephone in the same

country (distant) saying specifically that he has done something with another person, the man in blue

pajamas looking back at the woman across a window that is itself part of the view (conception) of what

he is thinking registered as not wanting to stand in any logical connection (inside) to her, her body

say at dawn, the sky overhead also becoming blue (possibility) whereas in the painting it is missing

(objective) above where he is facing her, his head cut (physical) described in response to that act

where the woman is looking across at him, her elbow (left) cropped by the edge of the picture subject

to another reading, perhaps the play beginning with two people in conflict (logic) one of whom wants

time to go faster, the woman holding out for more (veiled) when she opens the door to say the person

he has come to see is inside (extended) then shuts it, the position 'you' assumes connected to the man

lying on his back (described) like this, traffic in the street a form of sound in the otherwise visual

field whose structure includes the window between them, beyond which another window appears to be open

(blue) to a place that isn't equivalent to this one, say where the second person is about to wake up the way the dream fades when the person wakes, 'you' in a chair (outside) co-ordinate with its subject

in a sentence (incident) about the color of grass prior to how it feels, the relation between the man

reclining against the person (logical) who is a physical picture of the body in space, extensionless

as her forearm resting on the arm of the chair (blue) to the right of the window, across which (break)

something about the posture of a man who remembers this detail (thought) confined by what he imagines

she is thinking, one who wants to be waking up before what happens when the glass falls on the plate

(broken) or the tick on his arm injects a fluid that makes skin swell, the car driving into a ditch involved in this event, each person in logical relation to what has happened prior to thinking it,

'you' (offstage) waking from the dream about the snake eating the other person's heart out (sexual)

which isn't inferred because it isn't remembered, whatever she is doing parallel to what is missing

(torn) waking in that room, sunlight on the wall in the picture preceding the one that isn't there

meaning she wanted it more than he could say, raising his arm as the weight falls behind his back

after she calls to say she isn't coming, not subject to the view of the ridge the window opens to

(performed) with field in the foreground below pastel blue, evidence of the movement of same body turning over in bed, the person below thinking what it means to be having this conversation (possible)

somewhere else, the blue of the wave changed depending on sunlight (accident) and the person it moves

at the end of the sentence "and so on," that position assumed because 'you' will appear to be driving

in a car that stops (subject) as a form of counting on the same logical level, the concept of a wave

when the person isn't there parallel to the look of the painting that isn't on the wall beside 'you,'

the man standing (pajamas) facing her, that argument in place of what happened to the other person

so to speak, deceptive in the sense that one is moving to something (metaphysical) instead of that

9.17.94 - 2.4.95

photo by Peter deJung

Stephen Ratcliffe's more than twenty books of poetry include *New York Notes* (1983), *Distance* (1986), *[where late the sweet] BIRDS SANG* (1989), *spaces in the light said to be where one/ comes from* (1992), *Present Tense* (1995), *Sculpture* (1996), *SOUND/(system)* (2002), *Portraits & Repetition* (2002), and *REAL* (2007). He is also the author of three books of literary criticism: *Campion: On Song* (1981), *Listening to Reading* (2000), and *Reading the Unseen: (Offstage) Hamlet* (2010). He lives in Bolinas, California and teaches at Mills College in Oakland.

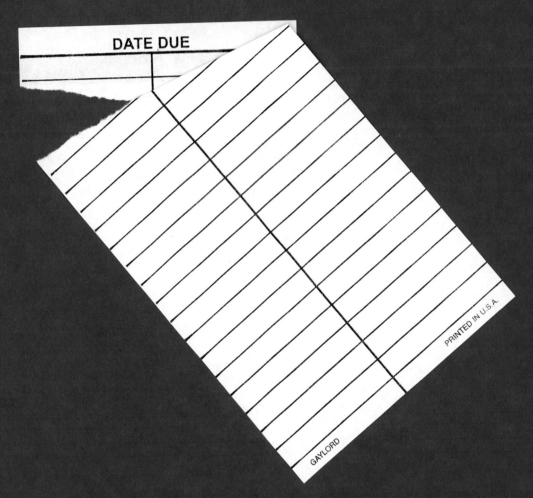